Code with Conscience:
The Importance of Humanising AI

Introduction: AI – A Tool, Not a Tyrant

In the bustling corridors of innovation, where the hum of machines grows ever louder, there's a new player that's been making quite the racket: Artificial Intelligence. But before we get carried away, let's set the record straight. This isn't a tale of robots taking over the world, nor is it a sci-fi fantasy where humanity bows to its digital overlords. No, this is a story of partnership, of balance, and of a tool that, when wielded correctly, can usher in an era of unprecedented progress.

Chris Williams, the voice guiding you through these pages, has always championed a simple, yet profound mantra: "AI is just a tool to help, it's not a replacement of!" It's a sentiment that resonates deeply, especially in a world where every Tom, Dick, and Harry seems to think that AI is the answer to all our prayers. But let's not kid ourselves. Like any tool, from the humble hammer to the intricate computer, AI is only as good as the hands that wield it.

You might've heard the saying, "AI will not take your job, someone using AI will." It's a cheeky reminder that AI, in itself, isn't the threat. The real danger lies in how we use it, how we integrate it into our societies, and how we let it influence our decisions. Left unchecked, AI could very well be the spark that ignites World War Three or, even more ominously, the end of humanity as we know it. Sounds a bit dramatic, doesn't it? But the stakes are indeed that high.

This book isn't just a guide to understanding AI; it's a clarion call to ensure that as we march forward into this brave new world, we do so with our eyes wide open and our moral compass firmly in hand. The human touch, that ineffable quality that makes us laugh, cry, dream, and hope, must remain at the heart of AI. It's our insurance policy against letting AI run amok. It's our guarantee that the machines we build reflect our best qualities, not our worst.

In recent times, there's been a rather concerning trend emerging. The digital landscape has seen a surge of 'hit and hope' marketers, those who, with a glint in their eye, see AI not as a tool for progress, but as a quick route to line their pockets. They peddle courses, webinars, and 'masterclasses', teaching the masses how to exploit tools like ChatGPT and its kin. The promise? A swift quid with minimal effort. But at what cost?

The misuse of AI in such a manner isn't just a question of ethics; it's a reflection of a deeper societal issue. When powerful tools are used recklessly, without understanding or respect, the ripple effects can be profound. It dilutes the genuine potential of AI, turning what could be a force for good into a mere gimmick. Moreover, it raises questions about responsibility. In a world where information is power, should we not be more discerning about how we wield and share that power? The unchecked propagation of AI for short-term gains risks overshadowing its long-term benefits, muddying the waters for those genuinely seeking to harness its potential for positive change.

In the chapters that follow, we'll explore the wonders of AI, its potential pitfalls, and the critical importance of humanising it. Because, at the end of the day, AI should serve us, not the other way around. And as long as we approach it with a sense of morality, ethics, and a good dose of wit, we'll ensure that the future is not just bright, but downright brilliant.

Table of contents:

1. Introduction: A Brave New World

The Unstoppable March of AI: A brief overview

In the vast tapestry of human innovation, Artificial Intelligence stands out as a beacon of both wonder and trepidation. Its journey from the pages of science fiction, where machines pondered existential questions, to its pervasive presence in our daily lives, is nothing short of remarkable. But AI's influence extends far beyond the robots of popular culture or the voice assistants we've grown fond of barking orders at. It's the invisible hand guiding the algorithms that curate our entertainment, the sophisticated systems forecasting economic trends, and the cutting-edge tools aiding medical professionals in diagnosing ailments with precision once deemed the stuff of fantasy.

But to truly grasp the essence of AI, we must first answer a fundamental question: What is AI, really?

Artificial Intelligence, at its heart, is not just a buzzword or a singular technology. It's an umbrella term encompassing a myriad of techniques and tools designed to mimic or replicate aspects of human intelligence. It's about machines processing information, learning from it, and making informed decisions based on that knowledge—much like the human brain, albeit without the penchant for daydreaming or the occasional forgetfulness.

Learning and Adapting: One of the core tenets of AI is its ability to learn. Through machine learning, systems are trained using vast amounts of data, refining their algorithms as they process more information. It's akin to how we humans learn from experience, though AI can often do it at a much faster rate and on a grander scale.

Neural Networks and Deep Learning: Drawing inspiration from the human brain, neural networks are interconnected layers of algorithms that process information. The 'deep' in deep learning refers to the number of layers in these networks. The deeper the network, the more complex the patterns it can recognise. It's the difference between recognising that you're looking at a face and distinguishing whose face it is.

Natural Language Processing (NLP): Ever chatted with a virtual assistant or used a translation app? That's NLP at work. It's the domain of AI that focuses on the interaction between computers and humans through language. It enables machines to understand, interpret, and generate human language in a way that's meaningful.

Cognitive Computing: This is about creating a natural, human-like interaction with machines. Cognitive systems can interpret visual or auditory information, reason through it, and even exhibit emotional intelligence in some cases.

Robotics: While often what first springs to mind when one thinks of AI, robotics is but a subset. It's the branch that deals with the design and creation of robots—machines capable of carrying out tasks autonomously.

The past few decades have indeed witnessed an explosive growth in AI. With the advent of big data, increased computational power, and more sophisticated algorithms, the boundaries of what machines can achieve have expanded dramatically. But it's essential to remember that AI, in all its forms, is still a tool—one shaped by human hands and guided by human intentions.

The Here and Now: AI's Current Capabilities

As of this moment, AI is not just knocking on the doors of innovation; it's well and truly inside, having a cuppa. We're witnessing AI's prowess daily. Self-driving cars navigate our streets, learning from every journey they undertake. Healthcare has been revolutionised with AI-powered diagnostic tools that can detect diseases from medical images with astonishing accuracy, sometimes even outperforming seasoned professionals. In the realm of finance, AI algorithms predict market fluctuations, helping investors make informed decisions. Even in creative fields, AI is making waves. From generating art and music to writing scripts, the machines are showcasing their artistic flair.

Moreover, personalised experiences have become the norm, thanks to AI. Ever wondered how streaming platforms seem to know your taste in music or movies eerily well? That's AI-driven recommendation systems at work, analysing your preferences and serving you content that aligns with your tastes.

On the Horizon: The Future Beckons

But as impressive as these advancements are, we're merely at the tip of the iceberg. The horizon holds promises that might seem straight out of a sci-fi novel. We're looking at the potential of neural interfaces that could allow direct communication between the brain and computers. Imagine controlling devices or even communicating with others using just your thoughts.

In the medical field, researchers are exploring AI-driven personalised treatments. Instead of a one-size-fits-all approach, treatments could be tailored to an individual's genetic makeup, ensuring higher efficacy.

Furthermore, the convergence of AI with other technologies, like quantum computing, could lead to computational capabilities we've never seen before, unlocking problems previously deemed unsolvable.

However, with these advancements come challenges and responsibilities. As we stand on the cusp of these innovations, it's paramount to approach them with caution, ensuring that the human touch isn't lost amidst the digital whirlwind.

Why every business leader should give a toss about AI

In the ever-evolving world of business, staying ahead of the curve isn't just a luxury; it's a necessity. And right now, that curve is being shaped, moulded, and defined by Artificial Intelligence. But why should the captains of industry, the entrepreneurs, and the boardroom veterans sit up and take notice? Here's why:

Efficiency and Productivity: At its core, AI is a problem solver. It can sift through mountains of data at lightning speed, automating tasks that would take humans hours, if not days. From streamlining supply chains to optimising resource allocation, AI can drive efficiency, leading to tangible boosts in productivity. In a competitive market, this edge can be the difference between leading the pack and playing catch-up.

Data-Driven Decision Making: In the age of information, data is the new gold. But raw data, in its unprocessed form, is like an uncut diamond—valuable but not particularly useful. AI can analyse this data, identify patterns, and provide actionable insights. For business leaders, this means making decisions based on concrete evidence rather than gut feelings.

Enhanced Customer Experience: Today's consumers expect personalised experiences. AI-powered systems can tailor product recommendations, optimise marketing campaigns for specific demographics, and even predict future consumer trends. By understanding and anticipating customer needs, businesses can foster loyalty and drive repeat business.

Innovation and New Opportunities: AI isn't just about improving existing processes; it's a gateway to entirely new avenues. Whether it's developing innovative products, exploring untapped markets, or identifying novel revenue streams, AI can be the catalyst that propels a business into uncharted territories.

Risk Management: The business landscape is fraught with uncertainties. Market fluctuations, geopolitical events, and even global pandemics can throw a spanner in the works. AI can model these uncertainties, predict potential risks, and even suggest mitigation strategies. In essence, it's like having a crystal ball, albeit one grounded in data and logic.

Talent Management and HR: Believe it or not, AI has a role to play in human resources. From screening resumes to predicting which candidates are likely to be a good fit, AI can streamline the hiring process. Moreover, it can identify training needs, monitor employee morale, and even predict attrition, helping businesses retain their best talents.

Staying Competitive: Let's face it, if you're not integrating AI into your business strategy, you can bet your bottom pound that your competitors are. Adopting AI isn't just about keeping up; it's about not being left behind. In an interconnected global economy, complacency isn't an option.

Ethical and Social Responsibility: As AI becomes more integrated into society, businesses have a role to play in ensuring its ethical deployment. Misuse or unchecked use of AI can lead to public relations nightmares. Conversely, businesses that champion ethical AI can enhance their brand image, earning the trust and loyalty of their customers.

In conclusion, AI isn't just another tool in the business toolkit; it's rapidly becoming the toolkit. For business leaders, understanding and embracing AI isn't just a smart move; it's an imperative. As the chapters ahead will elucidate, while AI offers immense potential, it's the human touch, the ethical considerations, and the strategic vision that will determine its true impact.

The Perils of "We've Always Done It Like That": A Cautionary Tale

Picture this: It's the early 1990s. The business world is abuzz with a newfangled invention called 'electronic mail'. While many forward-thinking companies are quick to jump on the bandwagon, seeing the potential of instantaneous communication, there's a cohort of business veterans who are sceptical. "Why would we need email?" they scoff. "We've always done it like that," they proclaim, pointing to their trusty fax machines and the piles of paper memos.

Enter Company A and Company B. Both are well-established firms with a rich history and a loyal clientele. Company A, led by a visionary leader, decides to embrace email, training its employees and integrating it into their daily operations. Company B, on the other hand, led by a stalwart of the old school, dismisses email as a passing fad, sticking to their tried-and-tested methods.

Fast forward a few years. Company A's decision to adopt email has transformed its operations. Communication is swifter, decisions are made faster, and the company is able to respond to market changes in real-time. They've also expanded their client base globally, thanks to the ease of digital communication.

Company B? They're struggling. Their refusal to adapt means they're slower to respond to client queries, leading to frustration. Their international clients, accustomed to the immediacy of email, are jumping ship. And the younger talent, keen to work in a modern environment, are choosing competitors over them.

The moral of the story? "We've always done it like that" is not just a harmless phrase; it's a dangerous mindset. In a world where change is the only constant, adaptability isn't just a virtue; it's a survival skill. Just as those who dismissed the potential of email found themselves relegated to the annals of history, businesses that ignore the transformative power of AI risk a similar fate.

So, to the seasoned veterans of the business world, while experience is invaluable, it's essential to remember that the landscape is ever-evolving. And in this landscape, AI is not just a feature; it's fast becoming the very terrain.

2. The Evolution of AI: Philosophers to Terminators

In the grand tapestry of technological advancements, Artificial Intelligence stands out as both a marvel and a mystery. Its journey, from the realms of academic curiosity to the engine rooms of global enterprises, is a testament to human ingenuity and ambition. But how did we get here? How did a concept that once graced the pages of science fiction novels become a driving force in boardrooms worldwide? In this chapter, we'll embark on a nostalgic trip down memory lane, revisiting the milestones that shaped AI's trajectory. From its humble beginnings to the breakthroughs that left the business world agog, let's unravel the story of AI—one that's as much about human vision as it is about machine intelligence.

A Cheeky Trip Down Memory Lane: AI's Humble Beginnings

The story of AI isn't a recent one. While the term "Artificial Intelligence" was coined in the 1950s, the seeds of the idea can be traced back much further. Philosophers in ancient civilizations pondered the idea of artificial beings, and inventors from the Middle Ages dreamt of machines that could mimic human thought. But let's fast-forward to the 20th century, where the real magic began.

1. The Birth of an Idea: The 1950s saw the dawn of AI as a scientific discipline. The term "Artificial Intelligence" was first introduced by John McCarthy for the famous Dartmouth Conference in 1956. This gathering is often considered the birthplace of AI, where leading minds of the time, including Marvin Minsky and Claude Shannon, proposed that "every aspect of learning or any other feature of intelligence can in principle be so precisely described that a machine can be made to simulate it."

2. Early Adopters in Business: The 1960s and 70s saw businesses dipping their toes into the AI waters. Banks began using AI systems for tasks like cheque clearing, using character recognition to process vast numbers of cheques automatically. Airlines started employing AI for scheduling flights and crew, a complex task made simpler by AI's computational prowess.

3. The Pioneers: Several companies emerged as frontrunners in the AI race. IBM, with its Deep Blue chess-playing computer, showcased in 1997 that machines could outthink even the brightest human minds, defeating world chess champion Garry Kasparov. Expert systems, like MYCIN, developed in the early 1970s, were used in specific domains, such as medical diagnosis, showcasing the potential of AI in specialised fields.

4. The Winter and Revival: It wasn't all smooth sailing. The late 70s and 80s saw a period known as the "AI winter", where funding and interest in AI waned due to unmet expectations. But like any good story, there was a comeback. The 90s and early 2000s saw a resurgence in AI, driven by advancements in algorithms, increased computational power, and the availability of big data. Companies like Google and Amazon began harnessing AI for search algorithms and recommendation systems, setting the stage for the AI-driven world we live in today.

In these early days, AI was a blend of ambition, experimentation, and a dash of audacity. It was uncharted territory, and the pioneers were both visionaries and risk-takers. They saw not just what AI was, but what it could be. And while the journey had its share of bumps and detours, it laid the foundation for the AI revolution we're witnessing today.

The Game-Changers: AI Breakthroughs That Shook the Boardroom

While AI's journey has been marked by steady progress, there have been certain watershed moments—breakthroughs that didn't just push the envelope but tore it to shreds. These are the milestones that had boardrooms buzzing and reshaped industries.

1. Deep Learning Takes Centre Stage: In the early 2010s, a technique known as deep learning began to revolutionise AI. By using multi-layered neural networks, machines could process vast amounts of data and identify intricate patterns. This wasn't just a step forward; it was a quantum leap. Companies quickly realised that everything from image and voice recognition to complex decision-making could be enhanced by deep learning. The likes of Google, Facebook, and Microsoft poured resources into this area, leading to rapid advancements.

2. AlphaGo's Triumph: In 2016, the world watched in awe as DeepMind's AlphaGo defeated Lee Sedol, a world champion Go player. Go, with its near-infinite board configurations, was considered a game too complex for machines to master. Yet, here was an AI not just playing, but beating a human champion. This wasn't just a win on the board; it was a statement to industries worldwide: underestimate AI at your peril.

3. Natural Language Processing (NLP) Breakthroughs: The 2010s also saw significant advancements in NLP. Tools like OpenAI's GPT and BERT from Google showcased that machines could understand and generate human language with uncanny proficiency. Businesses saw potential everywhere—from customer service chatbots to AI-driven content creation.

4. Autonomous Vehicles Hit the Road: Companies like Tesla and Waymo began testing self-driving cars, turning the dream of autonomous vehicles into a tangible reality. The implications were vast, not just for the automotive industry but for logistics, urban planning, and more.

5. AI in Healthcare: Perhaps one of the most profound impacts of AI has been in healthcare. Tools capable of analysing medical images, predicting patient deterioration, and even assisting in surgeries began to emerge. It wasn't just about improving efficiency; it was about saving lives.

6. Personalised Marketing: The days of one-size-fits-all marketing campaigns were numbered as AI-driven analytics tools could segment audiences with unprecedented precision. Companies could tailor their marketing strategies to individual preferences, leading to higher engagement and conversion rates.

7. Supply Chain Optimisation: Companies like Amazon and Walmart began harnessing AI to predict demand, optimise inventory, and streamline logistics. The result? Faster deliveries, reduced costs, and happier customers.

Each of these breakthroughs wasn't just a technological marvel; they were disruptors. They challenged the status quo, forcing businesses to adapt or risk obsolescence. They showcased the boundless potential of AI, not just as a tool but as a transformative force. And as we'll see in the sections to come, this transformation is just the beginning.

Today's AI: More than just a fancy calculator

In the digital age, Artificial Intelligence stands as both a testament to our current achievements and a promise of what's yet to come. While today's AI showcases remarkable emotional acumen, creativity, decision-making prowess, and collaborative capabilities, the horizon beckons with even more tantalising possibilities.

In the Next Year: The immediate future of AI is about refinement and integration. We'll see AI becoming even more seamlessly woven into our daily lives. Think of virtual assistants that not only manage our schedules but anticipate our needs, perhaps even suggesting that afternoon break you've been skipping or reminding you to call a friend you haven't spoken to in a while. The emphasis will be on personalisation, with AI systems tailoring their responses and actions to individual users with unprecedented precision.

In 5 Years: As we move further into the decade, the boundaries between humans and AI will blur even more. We might see the rise of neural interfaces that allow direct communication between the brain and machines. Imagine composing an email or painting a digital picture using just your thoughts. In the realm of healthcare, AI-driven personalised treatments could become the norm. Instead of a one-size-fits-all approach, treatments might be tailored to an individual's genetic makeup, lifestyle, and even their microbiome, ensuring higher efficacy and fewer side effects.

In 10 Years: A decade from now, the AI landscape could be almost unrecognisable from today. We might be on the cusp of achieving Artificial General Intelligence (AGI) – machines that possess intelligence comparable to human abilities across the board. These systems wouldn't just be tools; they'd be collaborators, potentially even partners in creative endeavours. The business world might see the rise of AI-driven enterprises, where key decisions are made with the aid of AI, ensuring optimal outcomes based on vast amounts of data. Urban landscapes could be transformed with AI-driven transportation systems, reducing traffic congestion and environmental impact.

However, with these advancements come challenges. The ethical implications of AI will become even more pronounced. Questions about autonomy, rights, and the very nature of consciousness might move from philosophical debates to practical considerations. As we stand on the cusp of these innovations, it's paramount to approach them with both excitement and caution, ensuring that as we stride into the future, we do so hand in hand with our AI counterparts, guided by a shared vision of betterment and progress.

3. The Ethical Minefield: Navigating the AI Quagmire

In the exhilarating rush to embrace the wonders of Artificial Intelligence, there lies a treacherous terrain, riddled with pitfalls and challenges. This terrain, or 'quagmire' if you will, isn't just about technical glitches or software bugs. It's about the profound ethical and moral dilemmas that AI presents. As we grant machines greater autonomy and intelligence, we inadvertently wade into murky waters where the lines between right and wrong, just and unjust, become blurred.

The quagmire isn't just a result of what AI can do, but more pertinently, what we allow it to do. Every algorithm, every line of code, is a reflection of human intent. And with that intent comes responsibility. The decisions we make, the values we instil in these systems, will shape not just our technological landscape but our societal fabric.

Unchecked, AI has the potential to amplify biases, infringe on privacy, and even make life-altering decisions without transparency or accountability. But it's not the machine's fault; it's ours. As creators, developers, and users, the onus is on us to ensure that AI is developed and deployed with a strong moral and ethical framework. It's not enough to be dazzled by AI's capabilities; we must be its moral compass, guiding it with the same principles and values that we hold dear.

In this chapter, we'll delve deep into the ethical quagmire of AI, exploring the potential pitfalls, the cautionary tales, and most importantly, the imperative of a human touch grounded in ethics and morality.

The potential banana skins of unchecked AI

The world of Artificial Intelligence is akin to a vast, uncharted wilderness. It's filled with promise and potential, but like any wilderness, it has its dangers—areas where the unwary traveller might stumble.

One of the most treacherous terrains in this landscape is the inherent bias and discrimination that can creep into AI systems. These systems, after all, learn from data. And if that data carries the weight of historical prejudices, the AI, in its innocence, will adopt these biases as its own. We've seen this in facial recognition technologies that falter with certain ethnicities or in algorithms that inadvertently favour one gender over another. Such biases aren't just technical glitches; they're reflections of societal inequalities, and if unchecked, they risk perpetuating and even amplifying these disparities.

Then there's the ever-looming spectre of privacy. In AI's insatiable thirst for data, there's a danger of it becoming the digital equivalent of an overzealous detective, prying into personal spaces without consent. The tools that promise to personalise our experiences can, if not wielded with care, morph into intrusive snoopers, eroding the very essence of individual privacy.

But it's not just about what AI does; it's also about understanding why it does it. As these systems grow in complexity, their decision-making processes can become as convoluted as the inner workings of a human brain. And in this intricate web of algorithms and computations, accountability can become elusive. If an AI system makes a decision that has real-world consequences, pinning responsibility becomes a challenge. Is it the developer, the user, the company, or the machine itself that's to blame?

And of course, we can't ignore the economic ripples AI can create. It's a double-edged sword. On one side, it promises efficiency, automation, and progress. On the other, it threatens to render certain job roles obsolete. Without a thoughtful transition strategy, this can lead to economic disparities, with sections of society feeling left behind in the AI revolution.

In essence, the journey into the world of AI is not a simple trek but a complex expedition. It's filled with promise, but it also demands caution. As we navigate this terrain, it's crucial to be aware of these potential pitfalls, ensuring that our march forward is both progressive and principled.

Tales from the crypt: When AI went a bit pear-shaped

The journey of AI, much like any epic tale, has its share of highs and lows. While the highs are celebrated, the lows serve as cautionary tales, reminding us of the complexities and unpredictabilities of this technological marvel.

One such tale that stands out is the story of chatbots. These digital conversationalists, designed to mimic human interactions, were hailed as the next big thing in customer service and engagement. But not all chatbot stories have happy endings. A tech giant, in its enthusiasm, released a chatbot that was designed to learn from public interactions on social media. The idea was innovative: let the chatbot learn from real-world conversations to make its responses more authentic. However, within hours of its release, the chatbot began parroting racist, sexist, and downright offensive remarks. Trolls had quickly realised they could skew its learning, turning what was meant to be a showcase of AI's capabilities into a PR nightmare. The chatbot had to be pulled offline, serving as a stark reminder of the vulnerabilities of machine learning when left unchecked.

But chatbots aren't the only culprits. There have been instances where AI-driven hiring tools, designed to streamline the recruitment process, ended up perpetuating biases. One leading online retailer developed an AI tool to sift through resumes and shortlist candidates. However, because the system was trained on resumes submitted over a decade—a time when the tech industry was heavily male-dominated—it began to show an inadvertent bias against female candidates. The tool, instead of being an unbiased judge, became a reflection of historical gender disparities in the tech world.

Then there are the tales from the world of autonomous vehicles. The dream of self-driving cars is one filled with promise: reduced accidents, better traffic management, and a revolution in transportation. But the road to this future is fraught with challenges. There have been instances where autonomous vehicles, due to sensor misinterpretations or software glitches, have been involved in accidents. Each of these incidents underscores the complexities of entrusting machines with tasks as critical as human safety.

These tales, while sobering, are not meant to deter or disillusion. Instead, they serve as reminders. Reminders of the intricacies of AI, of the challenges that lie ahead, and of the need for a balanced approach that marries innovation with caution.

The moral compass: Why developers shouldn't just "wing it"

Imagine for a moment a bustling city in the not-so-distant future. The city council, in a bid to optimise public transport and reduce congestion, decides to deploy an AI-driven traffic management system. This system, named "OptiFlow", is designed to analyse real-time traffic data, predict congestion points, and dynamically adjust traffic light timings to ensure smooth flow.

On paper, OptiFlow is a marvel. In its initial weeks, the city sees a noticeable reduction in traffic jams, and the public is thrilled. But as weeks turn into months, certain patterns begin to emerge.

Residents of the affluent "Uptown Heights" neighbourhood, with its tree-lined avenues and luxury boutiques, enjoy consistently smooth traffic. The AI system ensures that their routes are always prioritised, with minimal wait times at intersections. However, the working-class district of "Downtown Groves", with its schools, hospitals, and markets, faces the brunt of traffic snarls. Ambulances struggle to reach hospitals in time, school buses are delayed, and daily commuters face longer travel times.

Upon investigation, it's discovered that OptiFlow was primarily trained on data from cities with demographics different from this one. The AI, in its quest for efficiency, had inadvertently prioritised routes frequently used by affluent individuals who, in the training data, often had vehicles equipped with the latest sensors. Downtown Groves, with its older infrastructure and vehicles, didn't fit the "optimal" profile the AI had learned.

The fallout is immediate. The city council faces public outcry, with accusations of classism and discrimination. The developers of OptiFlow, who had been basking in the initial success, are now on the defensive, trying to explain an oversight they hadn't anticipated.

This hypothetical scenario underscores a crucial point: AI development isn't just about technical prowess; it's a deeply ethical endeavour. Developers can't merely "wing it", hoping that the AI will figure things out on its own. Every decision, from the choice of training data to the deployment strategy, carries profound ethical implications. In the rush to innovate, it's essential to pause, reflect, and ensure that the systems we create are not just smart, but also just.

4. The Human Element: Not Just Another Cog in the Machine

In the intricate dance of progress, where machines whirl and algorithms dictate the rhythm, there's a danger of forgetting the most crucial dancer of all: the human being. As we stand on the precipice of an AI-driven era, it's easy to be dazzled by the feats of machine intelligence, to be lured into the belief that technology can, and should, take the reins entirely. But to do so would be a grave oversight, one that risks not only the efficacy of AI but the very fabric of our society.

Omitting the human element from AI is akin to removing the conductor from an orchestra. Without the guiding hand, the nuanced understanding, and the emotional depth that humans bring, AI systems risk becoming mechanical monstrosities, devoid of empathy and understanding. They might process data at lightning speed, but they'd miss the subtleties, the shades of grey that define human experiences. An AI system might excel in diagnosing a medical condition based on symptoms, but it might miss the anxiety in a patient's voice, the unspoken fears that a human doctor would pick up on.

But it's not just about the risks. Embracing the human element in AI brings a plethora of benefits. By ensuring that AI systems are designed, developed, and deployed with a human touch, we ensure that they remain grounded, relatable, and effective. A customer service chatbot that understands human emotions can provide comfort, a virtual assistant that recognises individual nuances can offer personalised experiences, and an AI-driven educational tool that adapts to a student's unique learning style can revolutionise education.

Moreover, by humanising AI, we ensure that technology serves us, rather than the other way around. It becomes a tool, an ally, a partner in our quest for progress, amplifying our strengths and compensating for our weaknesses.

In this chapter, we'll delve deep into the symbiotic relationship between humans and AI. We'll explore the dangers of sidelining the human element and celebrate the myriad benefits of ensuring that, in the world of AI, humans are not just another cog in the machine but the very heart of it.

Why robots can't replace the office tea round (and other human essentials)

The year is 2040. As you step into your office, the scene that unfolds might seem straight out of a sci-fi novel. Gone are the days of the familiar hum of conversation, the clatter of keyboards, or the aroma of freshly brewed coffee wafting through the air. Instead, a sleek robot receptionist, with its polished chrome exterior, welcomes you with a perfectly modulated greeting. It efficiently checks you in, its sensors swiftly recognising your face. Down the corridor, another robot, equipped with multiple arms, deftly sorts and delivers documents to various departments. In the break room, an AI-powered machine brews the perfect cup of tea, its algorithms having mastered the art of tailoring each brew to individual preferences. The future of work, it seems, has arrived.

But amidst this technological utopia, there's an unmistakable void. The warmth of human interaction, the spontaneous laughter shared over a colleague's weekend escapade, the camaraderie built over shared biscuits and impromptu tea breaks – all seem like relics of a bygone era.

Let's delve deeper into some of the futuristic scenarios that are currently the talk of the town:

Robot Caregivers: The ageing global population has led to a surge in discussions about robot caregivers. These aren't just machines that assist with physical tasks but are envisioned to be companions, equipped with sensors to monitor health, dispense medication, and even engage in rudimentary conversation. But can a robot, no matter how sophisticated, truly replace the gentle touch of a human nurse? Can it detect the subtle change in a patient's mood, offer a comforting word, or simply sit in silent companionship, providing solace with its presence?

AI Therapists: With the complexities of modern life, mental well-being has taken centre stage. Enter AI-driven therapists: always available, devoid of personal biases, and equipped with vast databases of psychological knowledge. They promise therapy sessions tailored to individual needs, based on patterns and data analytics. But therapy, for many, is a sanctuary—a space of trust, vulnerability, and healing. Can an AI, with all its algorithms, truly understand the labyrinth of human emotions? Can it offer the same safe space as a human therapist, whose empathetic nods and understanding silences often speak louder than words?

Virtual Companions: Loneliness, ironically in our hyper-connected world, is a growing concern. The solution? AI entities designed to be the perfect companions. They'd understand our preferences, remember our likes and dislikes, and always be there, a constant in an ever-changing world. But genuine companionship is built on shared experiences, on memories, on the ups and downs of life. It's about that friend who stood by you during tough times, the shared laughter over an inside joke, the comfort of a shoulder to lean on. Can a virtual entity, no matter how advanced, ever replicate the depth and richness of human relationships?

These scenarios, while technologically tantalising, underscore a fundamental truth: the essence of humanity is irreplaceable. It's not about resisting the march of progress or being averse to technological advancements. It's about understanding and acknowledging the limitations of machines. The office tea round, seemingly mundane, is a microcosm of human connections—the shared stories, the exchanged smiles, the brief respite from work. And while a robot might, technically, brew a flawless cuppa, it lacks the heart and soul that humans bring to even the simplest of interactions.

As we navigate the exciting yet challenging terrain of the future, it's imperative to remember that technology, in all its glory, should serve as an extension of humanity, not a replacement. Because some things, no matter how advanced our world becomes, remain quintessentially human.

Reading between the lines: AI's attempts at understanding us quirky humans

In 2018, Amazon had to scrap an AI recruitment tool because it showed bias against female candidates. The tool was designed to review job applications and shortlist the top talent. It was trained on resumes submitted to Amazon over a 10-year period. However, since the tech industry has been male-dominated, especially in the past, the AI system began to favour male candidates over female ones.

For instance, the system downgraded resumes that included the word "women's," such as "women's chess club captain." It also favoured resumes that had more male-associated terms, like "executed" or "captured." Even when Amazon tried to make the tool gender-neutral, there was no guarantee that the system wouldn't devise other ways to sort candidates that could be discriminatory.

This incident highlights the inherent challenges in training AI systems. While the AI was doing precisely what it was trained to do—identify patterns and make decisions based on them—it lacked the human ability to understand the broader context and the societal implications of its decisions. It's a stark reminder that AI systems, no matter how advanced, are only as good as the data they're trained on. If that data carries biases, the AI will inevitably perpetuate them.

This example underscores the importance of careful and considerate training data, as well as the continuous monitoring and refining of AI systems. It's not enough to simply set them up and let them run; there needs to be a human touch to ensure they're operating fairly and ethically.

Case studies: AI projects that didn't just rely on the on/off switch

In the vast tapestry of AI-driven innovations, certain projects stand out, not merely for their technological brilliance but for the seamless integration of machine intelligence with human intuition. These endeavours highlight the undeniable truth: the most transformative AI outcomes are birthed when technology is harmoniously married to the human touch.

IBM Watson in Healthcare: IBM's Watson is more than just a computational powerhouse; it's a beacon of how AI can revolutionise sectors like healthcare. Watson's prowess lies in its ability to trawl through mountains of medical data in the blink of an eye. But its crowning achievements have always been in collaboration with human experts. In numerous instances, Watson has put forth alternative treatments for complex diseases like cancer. While the AI churned out options based on vast datasets, it was the human doctors, with years of experience and intuition, who meticulously reviewed and validated these suggestions. They weighed the pros and cons, considered the unique circumstances of each patient, and made the final call. This blend of Watson's analytical capabilities and the doctors' seasoned expertise has led to groundbreaking treatments, offering hope and improved care to countless patients.

The Human Guardians of Autonomous Vehicles: The dream of cars that drive themselves, once confined to the pages of science fiction, is now a tangible reality. Companies like Waymo and Tesla are at the forefront of this revolution. But behind the algorithms and sensors lies a battalion of human experts. These professionals rigorously test and refine the AI systems, often taking to the roads to ensure the technology can handle real-world scenarios. They're the safety net, ready to intervene when faced with unpredictable situations. Their feedback is invaluable, helping to train the AI to be more adept and safer. This human-AI partnership is the cornerstone of the autonomous vehicle industry, ensuring that safety and innovation go hand in hand.

Blue River Technology's Human-Aided Agricultural Revolution: Agriculture, a profession as old as civilisation itself, is undergoing a seismic shift with the advent of AI. Blue River Technology is pioneering this change with its AI-driven solutions to identify and manage weeds. But this isn't a tale of machines replacing humans. On the contrary, human experts are integral to the process. They train the AI, feeding it data, refining its algorithms, and ensuring it makes decisions that benefit the crops. Their expertise ensures that the AI's precision is complemented by a deep understanding of the intricacies of farming. The result? Enhanced crop yields, sustainable farming practices, and a brighter future for agriculture.

Chatbots: The AI Front with a Human Heart: Step into the digital realm of any major corporation's customer service, and you're likely to be greeted by a chatbot. These AI agents, equipped with predefined responses and algorithms, handle a plethora of queries. But their true strength lies in their seamless collaboration with human agents. When a query becomes too complex or requires a touch of empathy, human agents step in, taking over the conversation. This hybrid approach ensures efficiency without compromising on the quality of interaction. It's a testament to the fact that while AI can handle volume, it's the human touch that provides depth, understanding, and genuine connection.

In each of these endeavours, the narrative is clear: AI, in all its glory, achieves its true potential only when complemented by human expertise, intuition, and ethics. It's a dance of progress where technology and humanity move in tandem, each enhancing the other, paving the way for a future that's not just technologically advanced but also deeply human.

5. The Nitty-Gritty: Making AI More Human

In the grand tapestry of technological evolution, AI stands out as a transformative force, reshaping industries, redefining possibilities, and reimagining the very fabric of our daily lives. But with this monumental power comes an equally significant responsibility: ensuring that AI remains grounded in human values, ethics, and sensibilities. And this responsibility doesn't rest on the shoulders of a select few; it's a collective endeavour, one that involves every individual connected to the AI ecosystem.

Designers are the architects of the AI experience. They craft the interfaces, mould the interactions, and shape the very essence of how AI systems present themselves to the world. It's imperative for designers to ensure that these systems are intuitive, empathetic, and reflective of the diverse tapestry of human experiences. An AI system that's well-designed is not just user-friendly; it's human-friendly, resonating with the emotions, needs, and aspirations of its users.

Coders, the wizards behind the curtain, breathe life into AI. Their lines of code are the DNA of these systems. It's crucial for coders to approach AI development with a deep sense of responsibility, ensuring that the algorithms they craft are free from biases, transparent in their workings, and aligned with ethical standards. Every line of code is a decision, and these decisions must be made with a keen awareness of their broader societal implications.

Users, often seen as passive recipients of technology, play a pivotal role in the humanisation of AI. Every interaction, feedback, and choice made by users shapes the evolution of AI systems. Users have the power to demand transparency, to question decisions, and to steer AI systems towards more human-centric paths. By actively engaging with AI, understanding its workings, and voicing concerns and suggestions, users become active participants in the journey of making AI more human.

In essence, the journey of humanising AI is a collaborative symphony, with each stakeholder playing a distinct yet interconnected part. It's a dance of progress where designers craft with empathy, coders develop with ethics, and users engage with awareness. Together, this collective ensures that as AI systems become more advanced, they also become more attuned to the intricacies, nuances, and richness of the human experience.

The future of AI is not just about smarter algorithms or more efficient systems; it's about creating technology that understands, respects, and enhances humanity. And this vision can only be realised when everyone comes together, united in the mission of making AI truly human.

The feedback loop: More than just a pat on the back

In the dynamic world of AI, the feedback loop stands as a pivotal bridge between users and developers, a conduit that channels insights, experiences, and perspectives. But it's not just about pointing out glitches or requesting new features. The feedback loop, when approached constructively and ethically, has the power to shape the very trajectory of AI's evolution, ensuring it aligns more closely with human values and needs.

Imagine AI as a fledgling bird, taking its first tentative flights. Each flight, each flutter of its wings, is an interaction with a user. And every time it returns to its nest, it brings back a treasure trove of experiences. This is where the feedback loop comes into play. It's the mechanism that helps the bird refine its flight, understand the winds better, and soar higher.

For users, every interaction with an AI system is an opportunity to mould its future. By providing feedback, they're not just pointing out the system's shortcomings; they're offering a roadmap for its improvement. Constructive feedback helps developers understand user needs, preferences, and pain points. It shines a light on areas that might have been overlooked, on nuances that algorithms might have missed, and on cultural or societal contexts that need to be factored in.

But it's not just about what the AI system is doing wrong; it's also about reinforcing what it's doing right. Positive feedback, acknowledging the system's successes, ensures that beneficial features and interactions are retained and built upon.

However, the ethical dimension of feedback cannot be understated. In the rush to make AI more efficient or more attuned to user needs, there's a risk of veering into unethical territories. Users, in their feedback, have the responsibility to ensure that their suggestions and critiques uphold ethical standards. For instance, requesting features that might infringe on privacy or promote biases should be approached with caution.

Developers, on their part, need to create mechanisms that not only encourage feedback but also ensure it's diverse and representative. An AI system trained predominantly on feedback from a narrow user base risks becoming myopic, missing out on the rich tapestry of global experiences.

In essence, the feedback loop is a collaborative dance, a continuous dialogue between users and developers. It's about co-creating the future of AI, ensuring that as it grows and evolves, it remains anchored in human values, ethics, and aspirations. It's a reminder that AI, in all its technological brilliance, is ultimately a reflection of its users. And with constructive, ethical feedback, users have the power to shape AI in an image that's not just smart but also deeply human.

Designing AI that doesn't throw its toys out of the pram

In the sprawling landscape of technological marvels, generative AI stands tall, wielding the power to create, innovate, and even mimic human-like outputs. But as we stand at this crossroads of innovation, it's crucial to remember that with great power comes even greater responsibility. The essence of this responsibility? Ensuring that our AI creations, while autonomous in many ways, are still tethered to a moral and ethical compass that we, as humans, provide.

Imagine, if you will, generative AI as a river. Left unchecked, it can overflow its banks, causing chaos and destruction. But with the right structures in place—dams, channels, and pathways—we can harness its power, directing it to benefit society. This is the role we play in the world of AI: the architects who shape its flow, ensuring it aligns with our collective values and aspirations.

Now, some might argue that AI, especially generative models, are too complex to be fully controlled. But that's a defeatist perspective. Yes, these systems are intricate, but they're not beyond our influence. Every algorithm, every neural network, every line of code—it's all crafted by human hands. And it's within our power to infuse these creations with our ethical and moral values.

How do we achieve this?

Diverse Training Data: Generative AI learns from data. By ensuring this data is diverse, representative, and free from harmful biases, we lay the foundation for an AI that understands and respects the vast tapestry of human experiences.

Ethical Oversight: Regular audits and reviews of AI outputs by dedicated ethical committees can ensure that the AI operates within defined moral parameters. These committees can act as the guardians of ethics, intervening when the AI veers off course.

Human-in-the-Loop: No matter how advanced AI becomes, there should always be mechanisms for human intervention. By keeping humans in the loop, we ensure that the final decisions—especially in critical areas—are made with empathy, understanding, and a broader societal perspective.

Feedback Mechanisms: Encouraging users to provide feedback on AI outputs ensures that the system is continuously refined. This feedback, especially when it comes from a diverse user base, helps the AI align more closely with human values.

Transparency and Explainability: Generative AI shouldn't be a black box. By making these systems transparent and explainable, we allow users to understand how decisions are made, fostering trust and ensuring ethical standards are upheld.

The narrative is clear; while generative AI has the power to shape the future, we, as its creators and stewards, have the responsibility—and the capability—to guide its trajectory. We're not mere spectators in the AI revolution; we're active participants, holding the reins, ensuring that our technological marvels reflect the best of humanity.

In the end, it's a dance of co-creation. And as we move forward, it's imperative to remember that while AI can suggest the steps, it's the human touch that provides the rhythm, the soul, and the direction.

The dream team: Why your AI project needs a Jane from accounting

In the bustling corridors of tech innovation, where developers and data scientists are hailed as the rockstars of the AI revolution, there's another unsung hero that often goes unnoticed: the end user. And while it might be tempting to think of AI projects as the exclusive domain of tech gurus, the truth is, overlooking the insights and experiences of end users—like our good old Jane from accounting—can be a costly mistake.

Why? Because at the heart of every successful AI project is a deep understanding of its intended users. Without this, even the most sophisticated AI system can end up feeling like a square peg in a round hole—technically impressive, but fundamentally misaligned with real-world needs.

Let's break down why Jane, and users like her, are indispensable to the AI development process:

Grounded Insights: While developers bring technical expertise to the table, end users offer something equally valuable: grounded insights. Jane, with her day-to-day experiences in accounting, knows the challenges, nuances, and intricacies of her job. She understands where automation can help, where human touch is irreplaceable, and where the pain points lie. By involving Jane in the AI development process, you ensure that the system is tailored to address real-world challenges.

Usability Testing: An AI system might be a marvel of engineering, but if it's not user-friendly, it's bound to gather digital dust. Jane, as an end user, can provide feedback on the system's usability, highlighting areas that are intuitive and pointing out those that are clunky or confusing. This iterative feedback ensures that the final product is not just powerful, but also a joy to use.

Ethical Considerations: End users, with their on-the-ground experiences, can offer valuable insights into the ethical implications of AI implementations. Jane, for instance, might highlight potential biases in financial algorithms or point out privacy concerns in data collection processes. By giving end users a seat at the table, you ensure that AI systems are developed with a keen awareness of ethical considerations.

Adoption and Advocacy: An AI system's success isn't just measured by its technical prowess, but by its adoption rate. By involving end users like Jane in the development process, you not only ensure that the system meets their needs, but you also create internal advocates—individuals who understand the system's value and champion its adoption within the organisation.

Continuous Improvement: The development of an AI system isn't a one-off event; it's a continuous journey of refinement and improvement. Jane, with her regular interactions with the system, can provide ongoing feedback, ensuring that the AI evolves in tandem with changing user needs and organisational goals.

In essence, while the tech wizards lay the foundation of an AI system, it's the end users who breathe life into it, ensuring it's aligned with real-world needs, challenges, and aspirations.

Ignoring the end user in the AI development process is akin to building a ship without consulting the captain. It might float, but will it sail smoothly to its intended destination?

6. The Bigger Picture: AI's Role in the world

Throughout human history, every epoch has its defining innovations—fire that illuminated the dark recesses of prehistoric caves, the wheel that set ancient civilisations in motion, the steam engine that ushered in the industrial revolution. Today, as we stand on the cusp of a new era, Artificial Intelligence emerges as the beacon that promises to redefine the contours of the modern world.

On the global stage, AI isn't just another technological marvel; it's a transformative force, reshaping economies, societies, and even the very fabric of human interaction. From the bustling metropolises of New York and Tokyo to the serene landscapes of rural Africa, AI's footprint is ubiquitous, touching lives in myriad, often imperceptible ways.

In healthcare, AI-driven diagnostics and treatments are revolutionising patient care, offering hope to those in remote corners of the world, previously untouched by advanced medical facilities. Machine learning models predict outbreaks, ensuring that resources are mobilised efficiently, saving countless lives in the process.

The environment stands to gain immensely from AI's prowess. Predictive algorithms monitor climate patterns, offering insights into the looming challenges of global warming. Innovative solutions, driven by AI, are emerging to combat pollution, manage waste, and harness sustainable energy sources, promising a greener, more sustainable future.

In the realm of economics, AI is both a boon and a challenge. While it promises efficiency, productivity, and unprecedented growth, it also poses questions about job displacement, economic disparities, and the future of work. Nations are grappling with these challenges, striving to strike a balance that ensures prosperity while safeguarding societal well-being.

Education, the cornerstone of societal progress, is being reimagined in the age of AI. Personalised learning experiences, driven by intelligent algorithms, ensure that students across the globe receive instruction tailored to their unique needs and aspirations. Barriers of language, distance, and economic disparity are gradually being dismantled, paving the way for a world where knowledge knows no bounds.

But with these immense possibilities come profound challenges. Issues of privacy, ethical considerations, biases in algorithms, and the concentration of AI power in the hands of a few corporations and nations are pressing concerns that the global community must address collectively.

As we navigate this brave new world, it's imperative to remember that AI, in all its glory, is but a tool—a reflection of its creators and users. Its trajectory on the global stage will be determined not just by lines of code or neural networks, but by the collective choices, ethics, and aspirations of humanity. In the end, the story of AI in the wider world is, in essence, the story of us—our dreams, our challenges, our hopes, and our shared destiny.

How AI can be the bee's knees for society

In the intricate dance of modern society, where challenges often waltz with opportunities, AI emerges not as a mere spectator but as a lead dancer, guiding us towards a future filled with promise. Much like the diligent bee, which flits from flower to flower, ensuring the cycle of life continues, AI has the potential to touch every facet of our lives, ensuring progress and prosperity.

Imagine a world where healthcare isn't just about treating ailments but predicting and preventing them. In this world, a mother in a remote village, miles away from the nearest hospital, can receive a diagnosis for her sick child through an AI-powered telemedicine platform. Surgeons, assisted by AI, perform intricate procedures with precision, reducing recovery times and saving lives. This isn't a distant dream but a reality we're inching towards, where AI becomes the guardian of our well-being.

As dawn breaks, and cities come alive, AI ensures they pulse with sustainability. It optimises energy consumption, ensuring lights only burn when needed, and public transport runs on routes determined by real-time demand. When nature unleashes its fury, AI-powered systems predict the onslaught, giving communities precious time to prepare and mitigate the impact. In this dance of urban life, AI ensures every step is in harmony with our planet.

In the realm of education, classrooms are no longer bound by four walls. A child in a bustling city and another in a tranquil countryside, separated by continents, embark on learning journeys tailored to their unique pace and interests. AI-driven platforms adapt, virtual tutors guide, and language no longer poses a barrier, thanks to real-time translation tools. Knowledge, in this AI-augmented world, knows no boundaries.

But it's not just about the tangible benefits. AI has the power to touch souls, to ensure that every individual, regardless of their abilities, has a voice and a place in society. For the differently-abled, AI-driven assistive tools open doors, both literal and metaphorical. They ensure that the world is not just accessible but also inclusive.

Economies, too, feel the positive tremors of AI's influence. Beyond the fear of job losses, there's a world of opportunity. New industries emerge, old ones are revitalised, and jobs we haven't even dreamt of become reality. Every economic uptick, every new opportunity, is a testament to AI's transformative potential.

And as the sun sets on our AI-augmented world, there's a sense of security, both in the digital realm and the physical. Cyber guardians, powered by AI, ward off threats, ensuring our data remains our own. On the streets, predictive policing ensures resources are where they're most needed, creating safe havens for communities.

Yet, amidst this dance of progress, there's a gentle hum, a reminder of our roots. AI assists in preserving the rich tapestry of human culture. Ancient manuscripts are digitised, endangered languages find new speakers, and art forms, on the brink of extinction, find new life through virtual recreations.

In this grand narrative, AI isn't just a tool or a solution; it's a partner, guiding society towards a future where challenges are met with innovation, and opportunities are accessible to all. It's a world where the dance of progress is inclusive, harmonious, and filled with promise.

AI: The bridge over troubled waters (and cultural gaps)

In the intricate mosaic of global society, where each tile represents a unique culture, nation, or belief system, the gaps between these tiles can sometimes seem insurmountable. Differences in language, traditions, values, and histories have, at times, led to misunderstandings, conflicts, and deep-seated prejudices. Yet, in this complex landscape, AI emerges as a potential bridge, a tool that can span these divides and pave the way for mutual understanding and collaboration.

> **Language and Communication:** One of the most tangible barriers between cultures is language. While learning a new language can be a daunting task, AI-powered translation tools are making real-time, accurate translations a reality. Imagine a world where diplomats, business leaders, or even ordinary citizens can communicate seamlessly, without the fear of misinterpretation. Such fluid communication can foster mutual respect, understanding, and cooperation.

> **Cultural Exchange Platforms:** AI can curate and recommend content from diverse cultures, allowing individuals to immerse themselves in foreign films, literature, music, and art. By experiencing another culture's artistic expressions, individuals can gain insights into their values, aspirations, and worldviews, fostering empathy and breaking down stereotypes.

> **Historical Contextualisation:** Misunderstandings between nations often arise from historical grievances. AI-driven educational platforms can offer unbiased, comprehensive histories, allowing users to see events from multiple perspectives. By understanding the past, nations can pave the way for a collaborative future.

> **Collaborative Problem Solving:** Global challenges, be it climate change, pandemics, or economic crises, require collective action. AI can facilitate collaborative platforms where experts from diverse backgrounds come together, pooling their knowledge and resources. Such collaboration can lead to innovative solutions and foster a sense of global community.

> **Social Media Moderation:** The digital realm, while a space for connection, can also be a breeding ground for hate and misinformation. AI-driven moderation tools can detect and curb hate speech, ensuring that online platforms remain spaces for constructive dialogue and cultural exchange.

> **Cultural Sensitivity Training:** For businesses and diplomats operating in foreign lands, understanding local customs and sensibilities is crucial. AI-driven training modules can offer insights into local etiquettes, traditions, and values, ensuring interactions are respectful and productive.

Predictive Diplomacy: AI can analyse vast amounts of data to predict potential flashpoints between nations or cultural groups. By identifying these in advance, diplomatic efforts can be directed to mediate and prevent conflicts.

In essence, AI has the potential to be the bridge that spans the troubled waters of cultural and national divides. By facilitating communication, fostering understanding, and promoting collaboration, AI can help weave a tapestry where every thread, no matter how diverse, is valued and celebrated. In this interconnected world, AI reminds us that while our differences define us, our shared aspirations and challenges unite us.

Big Tech's Responsibility to Society

In the sprawling digital metropolis of our age, the skyscrapers of big tech firms cast long shadows, touching every alley and avenue of our lives. These giants, with their pulsating data streams and humming servers, are the architects of our digital realm. Yet, as they sculpt the silicon skyline, there's an echoing call for them to recognise the weight of their influence and the breadth of their responsibilities.

The data they amass, flowing like the lifeblood of this digital age, is a treasure trove of personal stories, dreams, and secrets. As guardians of this new oil, these firms bear the solemn duty to protect it with unwavering vigilance. It's not just about erecting firewalls or thwarting hackers; it's a commitment to ensure that every byte of data is treated with the respect and confidentiality it deserves, shielded from the prying eyes of exploitation.

But their responsibility doesn't end with data. As they forge ahead, pioneering the frontiers of Artificial Intelligence, they carry the torch of ethical innovation. Every algorithm they craft, every neural network they train, must be imbued with a sense of fairness, transparency, and morality. In the vast neural labyrinths of AI, there's no room for biases or opaque decisions; the guiding light must always be ethics.

Yet, the digital realm they've built isn't just about bytes and bits; it's about people. And as the architects of this realm, they have a duty to ensure that its doors are open to all. This means championing digital literacy, ensuring that the tools and treasures of the digital age are accessible to everyone, from the bustling streets of global cities to the quiet corners of rural landscapes.

Their towering data centres, while marvels of engineering, also whisper of the environmental cost of innovation. As stewards of both the digital and natural world, big tech firms must tread lightly, ensuring that their carbon footprints are minimal, their energies green, and their practices sustainable.

In the interconnected corridors of social media, where the world comes to converse, they must also be the vigilant guardians of mental well-being. Recognising the challenges of screen addiction, the pressures of virtual validation, and the pitfalls of digital echo chambers, they must craft spaces that nurture minds, foster genuine connections, and promote mental health.

And as they navigate the global marketplace, their economic might must be wielded with fairness and responsibility. From ensuring that every employee, whether in gleaming headquarters or in distant supply chains, is paid a fair wage, to supporting local enterprises and paying their due taxes, their economic decisions must echo with integrity.

Big tech firms are more than just innovators or entrepreneurs; they are the custodians of our collective future. And as they sculpt the silicon skyline, the world watches, hoping that they rise to the occasion, ensuring that their edifices are not just monuments to profit, but beacons of progress, inclusivity, and ethical innovation.

7. Peering into the Crystal Ball: AI's Next Party Tricks

As we stand on the precipice of today, gazing into the vast expanse of tomorrow, the future of AI shimmers with possibilities, much like a mirage that's both tantalising and enigmatic. The AI of the future promises to be more than just lines of code or sophisticated algorithms; it beckons as a partner in our collective journey, evolving, adapting, and surprising us at every twist and turn.

Imagine a world where AI doesn't just respond to our commands but anticipates our needs, understanding our moods, aspirations, and even our unspoken dreams. It's a world where AI-powered companions offer solace to the lonely, guidance to the lost, and inspiration to the creatively parched. Beyond the realms of healthcare, finance, or entertainment, the AI of the future ventures into the uncharted territories of human emotion, spirituality, and consciousness.

Yet, as we peer deeper into this crystal ball, we also see challenges. The dance between AI and humanity becomes more intricate, demanding a symphony of ethics, innovation, and empathy. But one thing remains clear: the future of AI isn't just about technological marvels; it's a narrative of coevolution, where machines learn from humans, and humans, in turn, discover new facets of themselves through machines.

Predictions that don't require a magic 8-ball

As we navigate the currents of the present, it's only natural to cast our gaze forward, wondering what the morrow holds. The realm of AI, ever-evolving and ever-surprising, offers tantalising glimpses into futures both near and distant. While we don't need a magic 8-ball to foresee some of these advancements, the sheer potential of what's on the horizon is nothing short of magical. Here are a few predictions, grounded in today's realities, that paint a picture of a world where AI seamlessly intertwines with our daily lives, enhancing, enriching, and elevating our human experience.

> **Emotionally Intelligent AI:** Beyond just recognising human emotions through facial expressions or voice modulations, future AI systems will be adept at understanding the nuances of human emotions. These systems could offer personalised responses based on an individual's emotional state, providing comfort during distress, motivation during slumps, or even companionship to the lonely. Imagine a virtual therapist that can provide immediate emotional support or an AI companion that knows just how to cheer you up after a tough day.

> **AI-driven Personal Health Monitors:** Wearable technology will evolve to a point where AI-powered devices continuously monitor our health metrics in real-time, predicting potential health issues before they become critical. These devices could alert users to changes in their vitals, recommend dietary adjustments based on

detected deficiencies, or even schedule doctor's appointments proactively if they detect anomalies.

AI-enhanced Creativity Tools: While AI tools today can generate art, music, or literature, the future will see systems that collaborate with humans in the creative process. An author could have an AI co-writer suggesting plot twists, a musician could have an AI partner recommending chord progressions, or a painter could use AI to simulate how different techniques would look on canvas. These tools won't replace human creativity but will augment and enhance it.

AI Urban Planning and Infrastructure: Cities of the future might be designed with the help of AI systems that can simulate years of wear and tear, population growth, and environmental changes in mere days. These systems could recommend infrastructure designs that are sustainable, efficient, and resilient, ensuring that urban spaces are prepared for the challenges of the future.

Decentralised AI-driven Education: The classrooms of the future might not be bound by physical spaces. AI-driven platforms could offer personalised education to anyone, anywhere, adapting to individual learning styles and pacing. These systems could identify a student's strengths and weaknesses, offering additional resources or challenges as needed, ensuring that education is truly tailored to the individual.

These predictions, while speculative, are grounded in the advancements we're witnessing today. As technology continues to evolve, the line between what's possible and what's fantastical will undoubtedly continue to blur.

Guardians of the Digital Frontier: Ensuring Ethical AI Evolution

The digital landscape, with its vast potential and rapid advancements, is becoming increasingly dominated by the footprints of AI. As these footprints deepen and spread, the ethical terrain of this new frontier becomes ever more complex. The challenges and dilemmas springing from AI's integration into our lives aren't just technological; they're profoundly moral and societal.

Tech leaders, governments, and global organisations find themselves at the helm of this evolution. Their role isn't merely to champion innovation but to ensure that the path AI treads is one that aligns with the broader good of humanity. The exhilaration of AI's capabilities, from its data processing prowess to its predictive accuracy, is tempered by concerns about its ethical implications. Data privacy, algorithmic biases, and the broader ramifications of machines making autonomous decisions are just the tip of the iceberg.

Crafting a universally accepted ethical framework for AI is a monumental challenge. The diversity of human values, shaped by cultural, societal, and individual nuances, means that what's deemed ethical in one context might be contentious in another. Yet, the urgency for some foundational ethical principles is palpable. These principles wouldn't just serve as guidelines but as the very bedrock upon which AI's future is built.

Transparency is another cornerstone in this ethical edifice. The mystique of AI, where complex algorithms often operate in obscurity, needs to be replaced with clarity. It's not just about trust; it's about accountability. When an AI-driven medical system offers a diagnosis or a financial AI tool makes investment recommendations, the logic behind these decisions should be discernible. This transparency ensures that when AI errs—as all systems, human or machine, occasionally do—those errors can be understood, rectified, and learned from.

The task of shaping AI's ethical trajectory isn't one that can be shouldered by a single entity. It demands a symphony of voices—from the tech industry to academia, from policymakers to civil society. Each brings a unique perspective, and it's in this confluence of views that the most robust and holistic ethical strategies for AI can emerge. Collaboration isn't just beneficial; it's imperative.

The journey ahead, as AI continues to weave itself into the fabric of our daily lives, is uncharted. But with diligent guardianship, a commitment to ethics, and a spirit of collaboration, the digital frontier can be one where AI not only thrives but also serves as a benevolent force, enhancing and elevating the human experience.

Harmonising Silicon with Soul: The Indispensable Human Element in AI's Future

In the symphony of progress, where the rhythm of silicon beats in tandem with the pulse of humanity, a profound truth emerges: AI, for all its brilliance, is but a reflection of the human spirit. As we stand at the crossroads of a future shaped by both man and machine, it becomes evident that the essence of humanity—our empathy, creativity, and intricate decision-making—remains irreplaceable.

The digital neurons of AI, while capable of processing vast amounts of data at lightning speeds, lack the innate human ability to feel, to understand the nuances of emotion, and to connect on a deeply personal level. Consider the realm of healthcare: an AI system might diagnose with unparalleled accuracy, but it's the human touch, the comforting words of a doctor, and the empathetic gaze that often play a pivotal role in a patient's healing journey.

Similarly, in the world of arts and creativity, while AI can produce melodies, craft verses, and paint canvases, the depth of human emotion, the stories of our joys, sorrows, hopes, and dreams, are what give art its soul. An AI might replicate the brush strokes of Van Gogh, but can it capture the tumultuous emotions that birthed 'Starry Night'?

Complex decision-making, especially in scenarios laden with ethical implications, is another arena where the human touch is paramount. AI can provide data-driven insights, but the moral compass, the weighing of right and wrong, and the understanding of broader societal implications are inherently human faculties. Whether it's a judge delivering a verdict, a leader making policy decisions, or a parent choosing what's best for their child, the depth and breadth of human experience play a crucial role.

Yet, it's not about sidelining AI but recognising the potential of a harmonious partnership. When the analytical prowess of AI merges with the emotional intelligence of humans, the possibilities are boundless. From collaborative art projects where AI and artists co-create masterpieces to decision-making platforms where AI's data-driven insights are tempered with human ethics, the synergy between silicon and soul can usher in an era of innovations that are not only groundbreaking but also deeply humane.

In this dance of progress, as AI and humanity waltz together, it's evident that while AI might be the melody, the human spirit remains the soulful lyrics, making the song complete.

8. A Gentle Nudge for the Business Boffins

In the dynamic world of business, adaptability isn't just a virtue; it's a lifeline. As markets evolve and consumer behaviours shift, there emerges a clear differentiator between businesses that thrive and those that merely survive: the willingness to embrace change. And today, that change is epitomised by Artificial Intelligence. For the astute business leader, AI isn't a distant horizon to ponder upon; it's the immediate landscape to navigate. Embracing AI is no longer about gaining a competitive edge—it's about ensuring relevance, fostering innovation, and securing a place in the future of industry. In this era, where data drives decisions and automation amplifies outcomes, sidelining AI isn't just a missed opportunity; it's a strategic misstep. So, to the visionaries, the trailblazers, and the leaders: the future beckons, and AI is your compass. Will you heed the call?

The ABCs of ethical AI (without the jargon)

A - Awareness: Before diving into the AI pool, it's crucial to be aware of the ethical implications. This means understanding that AI, while powerful, can have unintended consequences. Start by educating your team about the potential biases in AI, the importance of data privacy, and the broader societal impacts of AI decisions.

B - Balance: AI is a tool, not a replacement. Ensure that there's a balance between automated decisions and human oversight. While AI can process vast amounts of data quickly, human intuition, empathy, and ethical reasoning should guide its outputs, especially in critical decision-making areas.

C - Consistency: Ethical standards shouldn't be a one-off checklist but a consistent part of your AI strategy. Regularly review and update your AI systems to ensure they align with these standards. This includes checking for biases, ensuring transparency, and validating the fairness of AI outputs.

D - Diversity: Ensure that the team working on your AI projects is diverse. Different backgrounds and perspectives can help in identifying potential biases and ethical pitfalls. A diverse team is more likely to create AI systems that are fair and representative.

E - Engagement: Engage with stakeholders, including employees, customers, and even the wider public, to gather feedback on your AI systems. Open dialogue can highlight potential ethical concerns and areas for improvement.

F - Flexibility: The world of AI is ever-evolving, and so are its ethical considerations. Be flexible and willing to adapt your strategies as new challenges and insights emerge. This might mean updating algorithms, retraining models, or even pausing certain AI functions.

G - Governance: Establish a clear governance structure for your AI initiatives. This should include guidelines for data usage, protocols for addressing AI errors, and a framework for ethical decision-making. Having a dedicated ethics board or committee can also be beneficial.

By following these ABCs (and extending to G!), businesses can ensure that their AI initiatives are not only effective but also ethically sound. Remember, ethical AI isn't just about avoiding pitfalls; it's about harnessing AI's power responsibly to create a positive impact.

Handy tools for the discerning business leader

In modern business, tools and technologies serve as the threads weaving success stories. As Artificial Intelligence continues its march into the corporate realm, it's not just about big concepts and grand strategies; it's also about the tangible tools that bring AI's promise to life. For the forward-thinking business leader, these aren't mere software applications but essential allies in navigating the competitive landscape. Whether you're looking to enhance customer interactions, streamline operations, or glean deeper insights from your data, there's an AI tool tailored for the task. So, without further ado, let's delve into some of the game-changing tools that are reshaping industries and redefining success in the AI era. Here are some tools that, possibly, by the time of print, may even be obsolete, that is the speed of tech advancements currently.

Data Analytics & Business Intelligence:

Tableau: A powerful data visualisation tool that integrates with AI to provide predictive analytics.
IBM Watson Analytics: Offers AI-driven data analysis and visualisation for business insights.

Customer Relationship Management (CRM):

Salesforce Einstein: An AI layer on Salesforce's CRM platform, offering predictive lead scoring, chatbots, and more.
HubSpot: While primarily a CRM, it has AI features that help in lead prediction and customer behaviour analysis.

Marketing Automation:

Adobe Sensei: Uses AI to offer personalised marketing solutions, content recommendations, and more.
Optimizely: An experimentation platform that uses machine learning to optimise marketing campaigns.

Chatbots & Customer Support:

Intercom: Offers a chatbot that uses AI to answer customer queries and direct them to relevant resources.
Zendesk Answer Bot: An AI-driven bot that helps customers find answers quickly.

Human Resources & Recruitment:

Pymetrics: Uses neuroscience-based games and AI to match candidates' emotional and cognitive abilities with company profiles.
HireVue: An AI-driven platform that analyses video interviews to evaluate and rank job candidates.

Supply Chain & Inventory Management:

Llamasoft: Provides AI-infused supply chain analytics and insights.
ClearMetal: Uses AI to offer end-to-end inventory visibility and demand forecasting.

Financial Analysis & Fraud Detection:

Kensho: Offers real-time event recognition and forecasting, helping financial professionals understand the potential market impact.
Darktrace: Uses AI to detect, respond to, and mitigate cyber threats in real-time.

Productivity & Collaboration:

Otter.ai: Transcribes meetings in real-time using AI, making note-taking a breeze.
Trello with Butler: Trello's automation feature, Butler, uses AI to automate tasks and processes within the platform.

Research & Content Creation:

Grammarly: Beyond grammar checking, its AI offers style, tone, and clarity improvements for written content.
MarketMuse: Uses AI to analyse content against competitors and offers suggestions for improvement.

The importance of not resting on one's laurels in the AI realm

In the ever-accelerating world of technology, AI stands out as a beacon of relentless progress. It's not merely evolving; it's metamorphosing at a pace that's both exhilarating and, for the unprepared, daunting. Yesterday's breakthroughs are today's norms, and tomorrow? Well, the horizon is as unpredictable as it is promising.

For businesses, this dynamism is a double-edged sword. On one flank, the opportunities are boundless. AI offers the chance to revolutionise operations, to create unparalleled customer experiences, and to tap into insights that were once the stuff of science fiction. But on the other flank lies the peril of complacency. In the AI realm, resting on one's laurels isn't just a missed opportunity; it's a ticket to obsolescence.

Consider the tech giants of yesteryears, the behemoths that seemed invincible. Many faltered, not because they lacked innovation, but because they failed to recognise the tidal wave of change until they were swept by it. In the AI era, such tidal waves aren't a decade apart; they're surging every year, sometimes even more frequently.

For the modern business leader, this means perpetual vigilance. It's not enough to implement an AI tool and then sit back, basking in its glow. Because, in the shadows, competitors are exploring the next iteration, the next advancement. They're harnessing AI's potential to not just improve but to reimagine and reinvent.

But it's not just about staying ahead of the competition. It's about serving the ever-evolving needs and expectations of customers. As AI reshapes industries, it's also reshaping consumer behaviours, desires, and demands. Businesses that fail to adapt, that rest on past successes, risk becoming relics in a world that's moving forward at warp speed.

In conclusion, while the allure of AI's current capabilities is undeniable, it's the promise of what's next that should keep businesses on their toes. In the AI realm, the journey is the destination, and standing still is simply not an option.

9. Conclusion: The Road Ahead (Without the Potholes)

In the vast expanse of human history, few moments have held as much promise and potential as the dawn of the AI era. As we stand at this unique crossroads, the path stretching before us is illuminated by the brilliance of Artificial Intelligence. Yet, this journey, as groundbreaking as it promises to be, isn't one AI can undertake alone. It requires a dance partner, and humanity is poised to take the lead.

The story of AI isn't just about algorithms, neural networks, or computational prowess. It's a tale of human ambition, of our ceaseless quest to push boundaries and transcend limits. AI, in its essence, is a mirror reflecting our desires, our dreams, and at times, our dilemmas. It learns from our past, acts in our present, and ventures into futures we've only dared to imagine.

But what makes this narrative truly enchanting is the undeniable synergy between humans and AI. Like two maestros in a grand orchestra, each brings something unique to the table. AI offers scalability, efficiency, and precision. It can sift through vast datasets in the blink of an eye, discern patterns beyond human cognition, and operate tirelessly. Yet, for all its marvels, AI lacks the human touch – the capacity for empathy, the intuition born of lived experiences, the ethical grounding that defines our very humanity.

This is where the captains of industry, the visionaries shaping our collective destiny, come into play. Their role isn't just that of spectators or beneficiaries; they are the custodians of this new era. As AI continues its march into every domain, from the arts to the sciences, from commerce to governance, its influence becomes omnipresent. And with great power comes profound responsibility.

For the business leaders of today and tomorrow, the challenge is twofold. First, to integrate AI into the very fabric of their enterprises, ensuring it augments human capabilities rather than replacing them. This means fostering environments where AI tools and human teams collaborate, where algorithms are guided by human insights, and where automation amplifies, not alienates.

Second, and perhaps more crucially, is the moral imperative. As AI's decisions increasingly impact lives, shape economies, and influence societal norms, ensuring its ethical grounding becomes paramount. Leaders must champion transparency, advocate for fairness, and constantly engage in the dialogue surrounding AI's societal implications. They must be the vanguards, ensuring that as AI reshapes our world, it does so in a manner that resonates with our shared values.

Moreover, the dynamism of AI demands unwavering engagement. The field is evolving, not in decades or years, but in months and weeks. New breakthroughs, novel applications, and unforeseen challenges emerge with startling frequency. For businesses, resting on laurels is not just risky; it's a recipe for redundancy. The clarion call for leaders is clear: Engage, innovate, and above all, ensure that the human essence remains at the heart of the AI revolution.

In the grand tapestry of the AI narrative, the threads of technology and humanity are interwoven in intricate patterns. It's a story of partnership, of mutual growth, and of a shared vision for the future. As we venture forth, the road ahead promises wonders and challenges in equal measure. But with the combined might of human spirit and AI's capabilities, there's no challenge insurmountable, no dream unattainable. The next chapter awaits, and together, we're poised to write a masterpiece.

10. The Utopian Future

In this concluding chapter, we embark on a visionary journey into a world where AI and humanity have achieved a harmonious coexistence. It's a future where technological prowess and human spirit have intertwined to craft a society that's not just advanced, but also compassionate, ethical, and inclusive. From cities that breathe and adapt, to workplaces that foster creativity and collaboration, to global communities bound by shared values rather than geographical boundaries, we'll explore the myriad possibilities of a utopia shaped by the perfect synergy of man and machine. Join us as we paint a picture of this idyllic future, offering a beacon of hope and inspiration for the path ahead.

As dawn breaks, the city of London awakens, bathed in a soft, radiant glow. The skyline, a harmonious blend of historic landmarks and avant-garde structures, stands as a testament to humanity's progress. Birds, both organic and AI-driven, serenade the city with a chorus that heralds a new day.

6:30 AM - Morning Routine

Len stirs as his smart mattress, embedded with sensors, detects the optimal point in his REM cycle to wake him. It adjusts its firmness, gently rousing him from slumber. Luna, his AI assistant with a personality matrix tailored over years to match his preferences, softly says, "Good morning, Len. Your biometrics suggest a light workout would be beneficial. Shall I set up the AR yoga session?"

Post-yoga, as Len steps into his bathroom, the mirrors assess his health metrics, offering insights and recommendations. By the time he's dressed, an AI-curated breakfast, balancing nutrition and flavour, awaits him. The ingredients, sourced sustainably, are prepared by his kitchen AI, which has learnt his culinary preferences over time.

8:00 AM - Commute

Exiting his apartment, Len steps into a London that's been reborn. The once grey and congested roads have metamorphosed into lush green corridors, with trees and plants absorbing carbon and releasing fresh oxygen. AI-driven urban planning has ensured optimal sunlight, green spaces, and pedestrian zones.

As he waits for his transport pod, he's entertained by AI-curated street performances – holographic artists playing instruments from around the world, a nod to London's multicultural essence. When his pod arrives, it's not just any pod; it's customised to Len. The seat adjusts to his posture, the ambiance inside the pod syncs with his morning playlist, and the windows turn transparent or opaque based on his preference.

The journey isn't just about reaching the destination. As the pod glides, it offers immersive experiences. Holographic news updates, curated to Len's interests, are projected. But it's not just reading; interactive AI journalists field his questions, diving deeper into topics he's curious about.

9:00 AM - At the Office

Stepping into his office is like entering a living organism. The walls, embedded with AI, greet him personally. Biophilic designs aren't just aesthetic; they're functional. Plants, monitored and nurtured by AI, purify the air, while the building itself adjusts its temperature and lighting based on the weather and occupants' comfort.

Luna, seamlessly transitioning from his home to his workspace, presents a detailed agenda on a floating holographic screen. But before diving into work, Len takes a moment in the AI-assisted meditation zone, where a serene environment is crafted based on his stress levels, ensuring he starts his day centred.

The collaborative project with the Tokyo firm is facilitated by an AI platform that not only translates but understands cultural nuances, ensuring smooth communication. It even simulates the ambiance of a Japanese office, complete with the scent of cherry blossoms, making the collaboration feel more personal.

12:30 PM - Lunch

Lunch is more than just a meal; it's a multisensory journey. The rooftop garden, a blend of nature and tech, is a testament to sustainable urban farming. Drones, guided by ecological AI, not only tend to plants but also provide insights into soil health, moisture levels, and optimal harvest times.

As Len walks through, he interacts with an AI botanist, learning about the origins of the plants and their benefits. He then selects fresh ingredients, which are immediately relayed to the kitchen. The chef, in collaboration with a culinary AI, crafts a dish that tells a story – of Len's past preferences, the current season, and innovative culinary techniques.

While eating, Len enjoys an AR experience where he sees the journey of his food, from seed to plate, understanding the symbiotic relationship between nature and technology in this utopian world.

3:00 PM - Afternoon Break

Len's relaxation pod is more than just a space; it's a sanctuary. As he steps in, AI sensors analyse his biometrics, detecting subtle signs of fatigue. The pod's interior morphs to create a beach setting. He feels the warmth of simulated sunlight on his skin, hears the gentle lapping of waves, and even senses the salty tang of the sea breeze. An AI-guided meditation voice, calibrated to Len's preferences, guides him through a deep relaxation session. By the time he emerges, he's not just rested; he's revitalised, ready to tackle the rest of the day.

6:00 PM - Evening Activities

Len's passion for understanding the deeper implications of AI leads him to a workshop on AI ethics. But this isn't your typical lecture. The room is facilitated by an AI moderator, which curates discussions, ensuring everyone's voice is heard. As debates heat up, the AI introduces real-world scenarios, challenging attendees to consider the ethical ramifications. It even simulates potential future scenarios, allowing participants to 'experience' the outcomes of different ethical choices.

8:00 PM - Dinner and Leisure

Tonight's dinner venue is renowned for its AI-human culinary collaborations. As Len enters, an AI maître d' recalls his past visits, dietary preferences, and even his recent activities to suggest a personalised menu. The meal is an experience, with each dish accompanied by a holographic story of its origin and inspiration.

Post-dinner, Len visits an art gallery, but this isn't just about viewing. It's interactive. He steps into art installations co-created by humans and AIs. In one exhibit, the artwork evolves based on the viewer's emotions, detected by AI. Another allows him to 'converse' with the art, exploring the artist's intent and the AI's interpretation.

10:30 PM - Nightcap

Back in the sanctuary of his home, Len retreats to his balcony. The city sounds are muted, replaced by a symphony of nature, curated in real-time by Luna based on his current mood and past preferences. As he relaxes, a holographic display, powered by an astronomical AI, paints the night sky, highlighting constellations, narrating ancient myths, and even offering glimpses into deep space phenomena. It's a perfect blend of science, art, and storytelling, ensuring Len ends his day with a sense of wonder.

In this detailed day, every moment of Len's life is enhanced by AI, not as a dominating force, but as a harmonious partner, amplifying the beauty, efficiency, and depth of human experiences.

As James's day draws to a close, it's evident that the utopian world he inhabits isn't just a product of advanced AI; it's the result of a harmonious partnership between humans and technology. Every facet of his life, enriched by AI, serves as a testament to the philosophy that AI is a tool designed to augment, not replace.

In this future, the fear of AI 'taking over' seems almost quaint. It's clear that AI hasn't taken jobs; rather, it has transformed them, elevating roles and allowing humans to focus on creativity, empathy, and innovation. The real power shift hasn't been from humans to machines, but from those who resist change to those who embrace and harness AI's potential.

The mantra resonates more than ever: AI won't take your job; someone using AI will. And in this utopian vision, it's evident that the 'someone' is a person who understands the symbiotic relationship between humans and AI, ensuring that technology serves humanity, and not the other way around.

In this world, AI isn't just a tool; it's a partner, a collaborator, and a reflection of humanity's aspirations. But at its core, it remains just that – a tool. And the true magic happens when that tool is wielded with purpose, ethics, and a touch of human brilliance.

www.ingramcontent.com/pod-product-compliance
Lightning Source LLC
Chambersburg PA
CBHW060010300526
45794CB00003B/1165